EXPLORE THE WORLD
LIFE SCIENCE

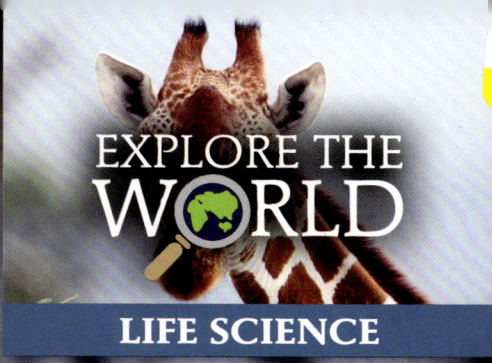

Boogers at Work

LAURA WHITE

TABLE OF CONTENTS

Mucus Mission 2
How Boogers Are Made 8
Flying Boogers 10
Why Does My Mucus Change Color?........14
Runaway Mucus 16
Glossary/Index 20

PIONEER VALLEY EDUCATIONAL PRESS, INC

MUCUS MISSION

If you've ever blown a snot rocket, had a cold, or picked your nose, you know that your nose can do both amazing and gross things. What you may not know is that the boogers in your nose, whether they're green and slimy or yellow and clumpy, have an important purpose.

3

Grown-ups usually call boogers **mucus**. Gooey, slimy mucus is a part of everyone's body. It moistens your food and makes it easier to digest. It coats and protects your stomach. It also acts like a protective blanket in your mouth, nose, throat, and lungs. Mucus prevents these important parts of your body from drying out.

Your nose produces about one cup of mucus every day.

MORE TO EXPLORE

Do you wake up in the morning with crusty eyes? That crust is actually a **THIN LAYER OF MUCUS.** You may not notice it when you are awake because it is cleaned away every time you blink. But when you sleep, your eyes are not blinking, so the mucus builds up and dries out in the corners.

Mucus acts as a **barrier** between the air and your mouth, nose, throat, and lungs. When air enters your nose or mouth, it brings in tiny bits of dust, dirt, **bacteria**, and pollen. These particles don't belong in your body. Mucus is like a spiderweb, grabbing the bits of dust, pollen, and germs that you breathe in. Once the mucus catches them, it wraps the particles in sticky goo to stop them in their tracks.

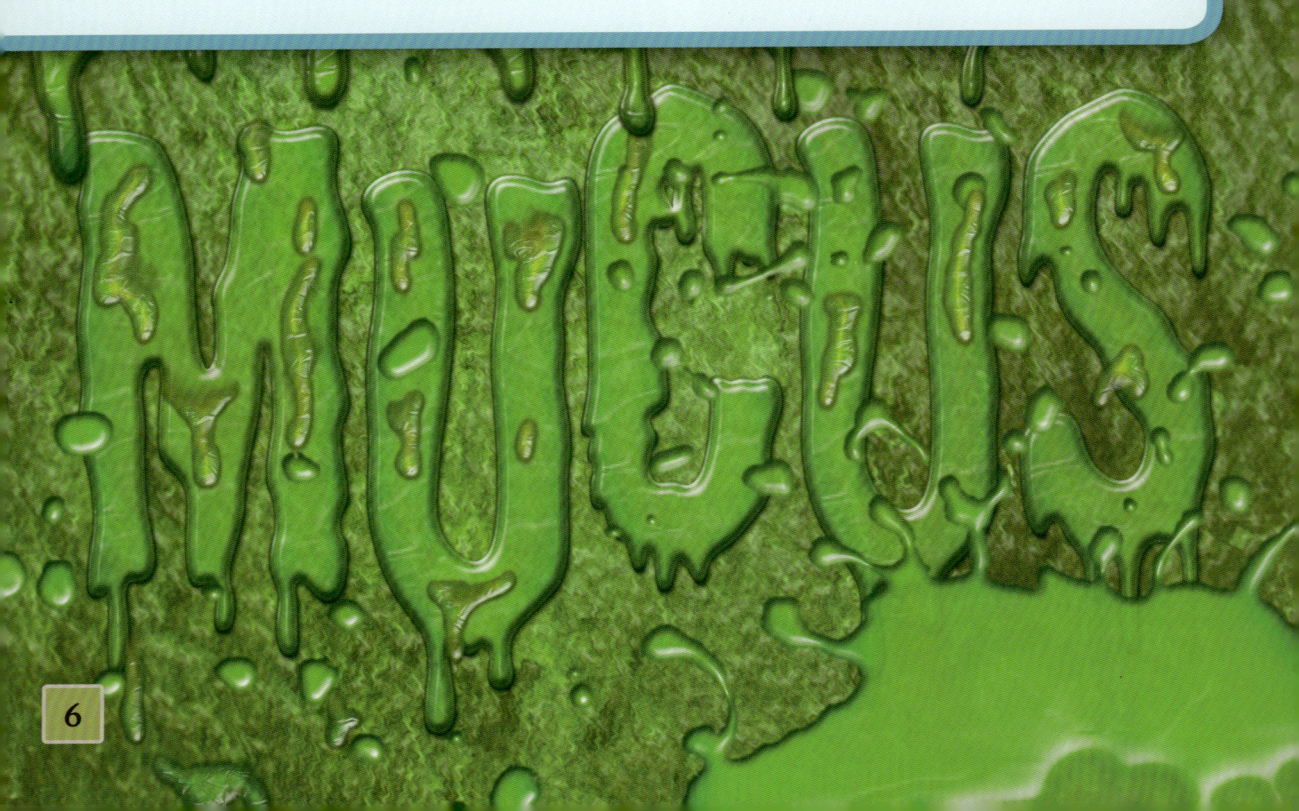

Because the particles can hurt your lungs and make it hard for you to breathe, mucus stops these particles before they can travel down your windpipe and into your lungs. By doing this, mucus keeps your body germ-free and healthy.

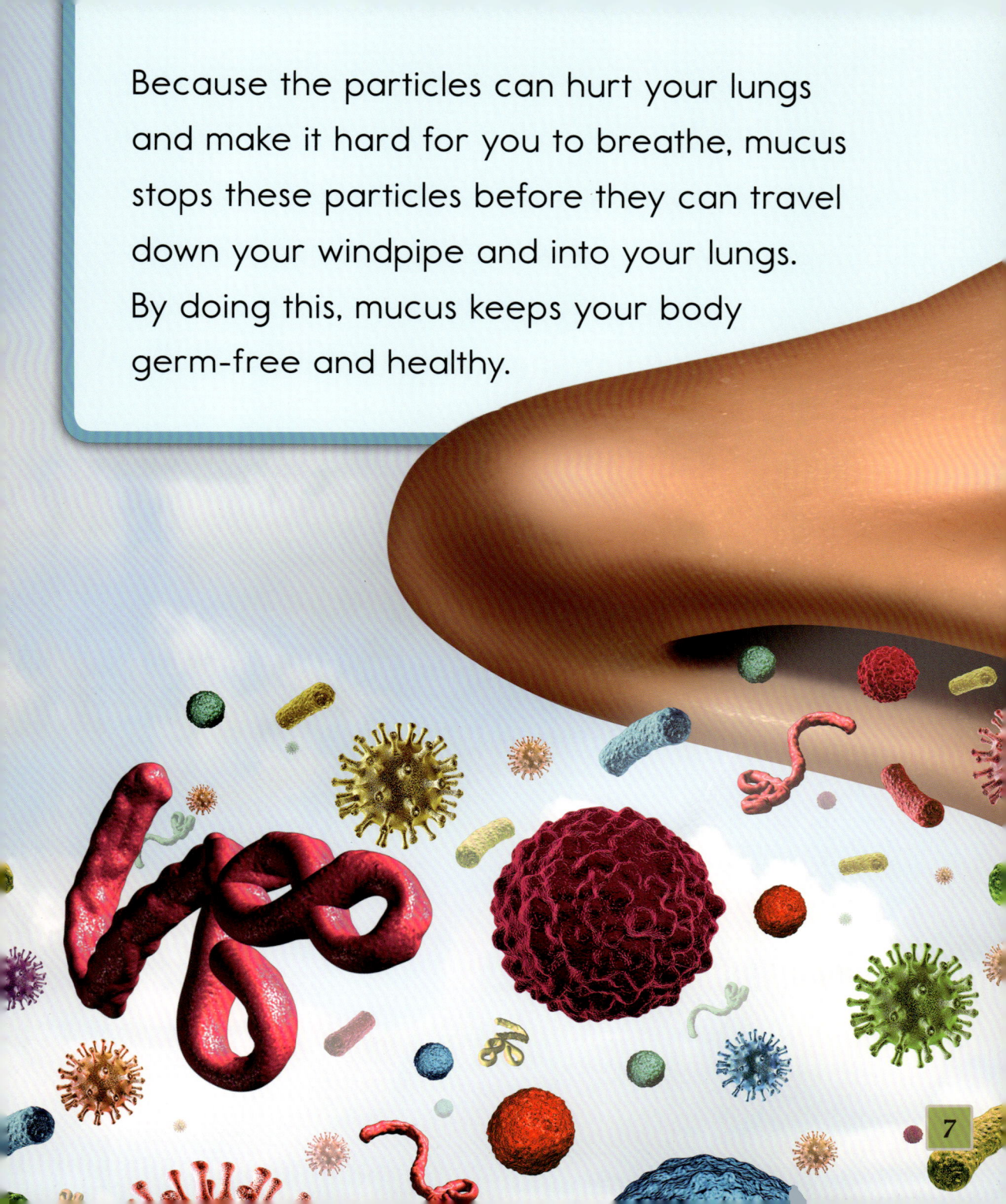

HOW BOOGERS ARE MADE

Once the particles are trapped in mucus, tiny hairs in your throat and nose called **cilia** sweep them away. The cilia in your throat move the particles back so that they can be swallowed. The acids in your stomach will then kill most of them. The cilia in your nose move the particles down toward your nostrils, where they clump together and form boogers.

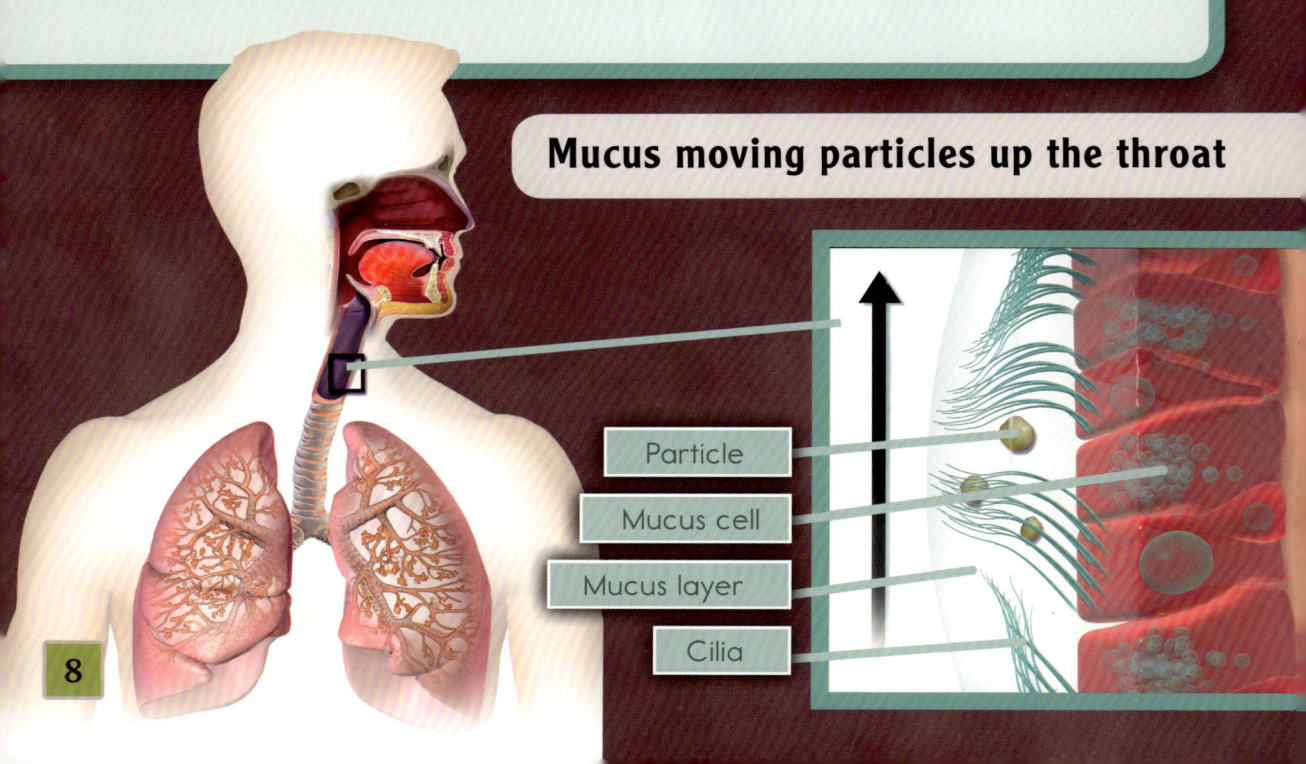

Mucus moving particles up the throat

Particle
Mucus cell
Mucus layer
Cilia

Boogers come in all shapes and sizes, but each one is pretty much just a sneaky bit of the outside world that tried to get into your lungs. Your body uses mucus to stop these invaders before they can do any harm.

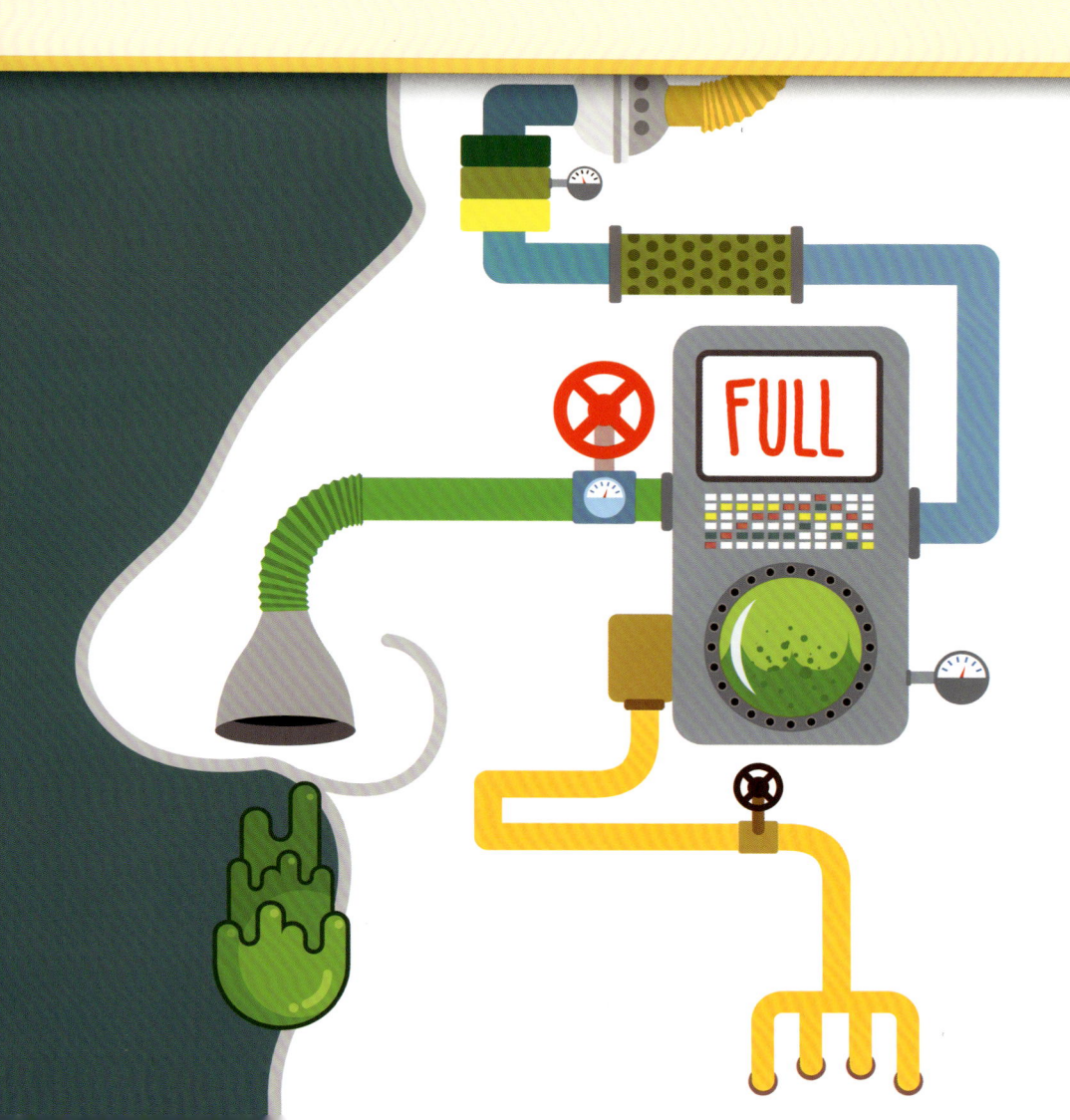

FLYING BOOGERS

When you blow your nose and **expel** the boogers, you are helping your body stay healthy. Blowing your nose is one way of removing particles that may cause harm.

Another way you can expel harmful particles is by sneezing and coughing. When germs and pollen enter your nasal passages, the cilia in your nose become irritated. This causes a tickling **sensation** in your nose. Your nose tries to clear itself by sneezing.

A good sneeze can blast air through the mouth and nose at 100 miles per hour. That's faster than most major league pitchers can throw a fastball! It's no wonder your parents tell you to cover your mouth and nose when you sneeze.

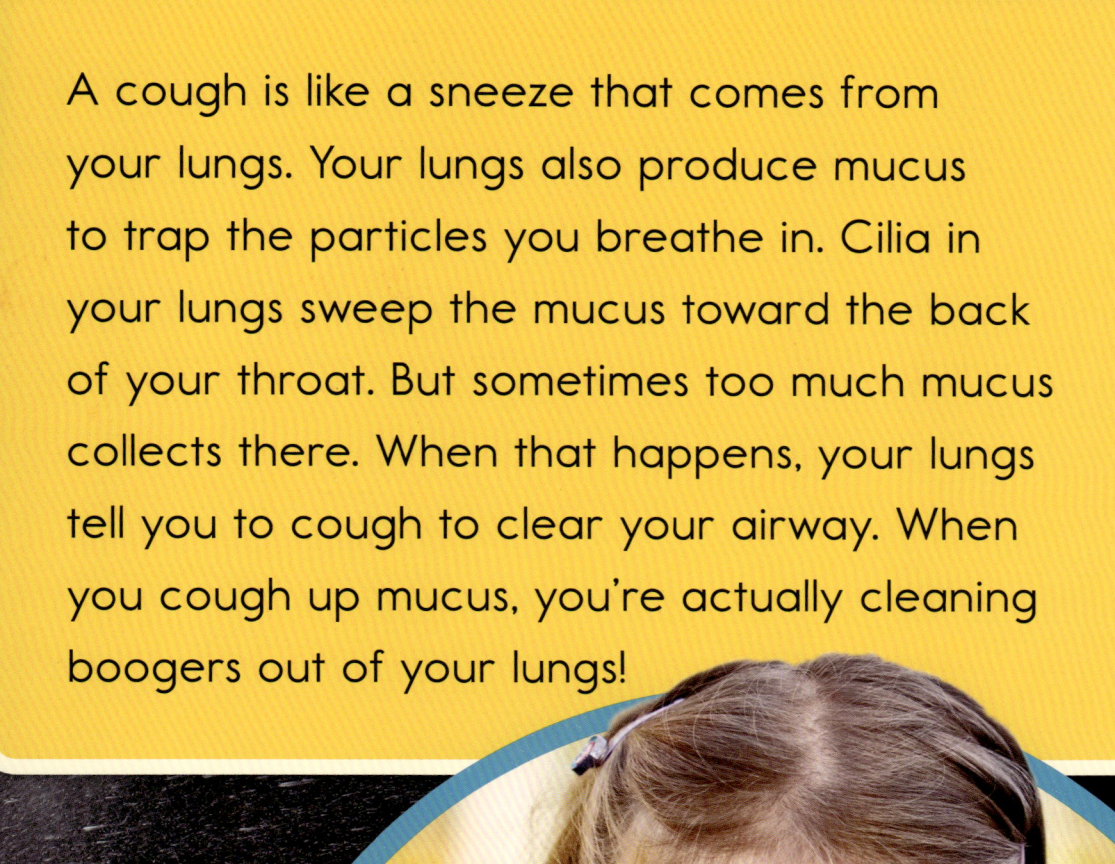

A cough is like a sneeze that comes from your lungs. Your lungs also produce mucus to trap the particles you breathe in. Cilia in your lungs sweep the mucus toward the back of your throat. But sometimes too much mucus collects there. When that happens, your lungs tell you to cough to clear your airway. When you cough up mucus, you're actually cleaning boogers out of your lungs!

WHY DOES MY MUCUS CHANGE COLOR?

If you look at your tissue after blowing your nose, you may notice that your mucus isn't always the same color. It may be yellow, green, or reddish brown. What do these colors mean?

Mucus turns yellow or green when you are sick. This is caused by white blood cells working to keep you healthy. The white blood cells produce a yellow-green chemical that kills germs.

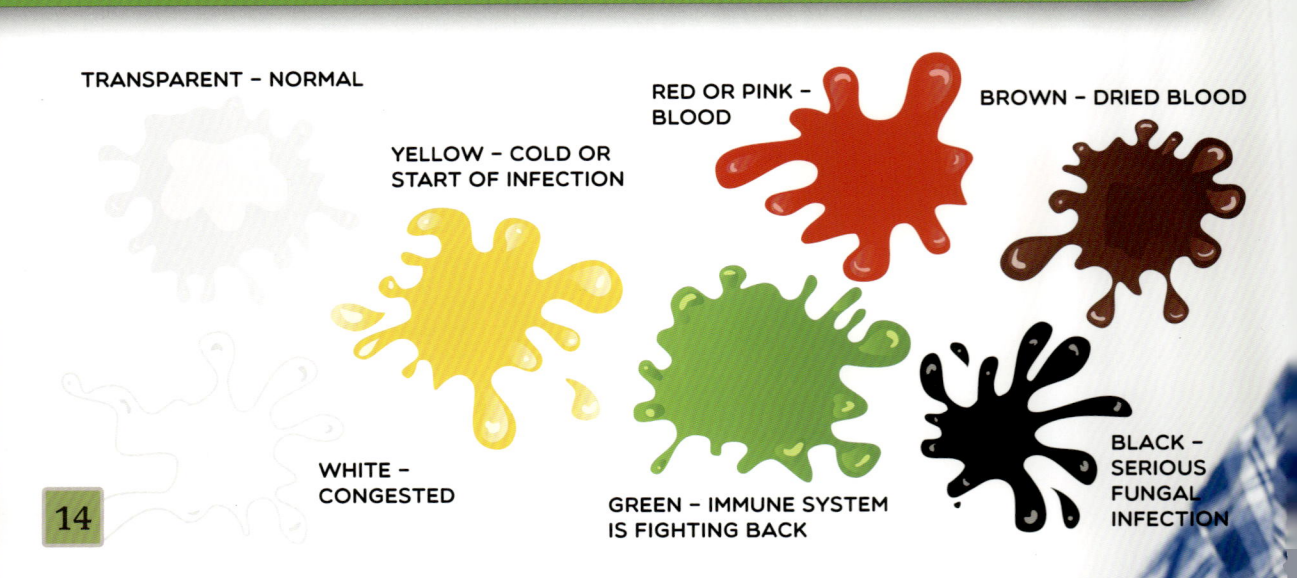

TRANSPARENT – NORMAL

YELLOW – COLD OR START OF INFECTION

RED OR PINK – BLOOD

BROWN – DRIED BLOOD

WHITE – CONGESTED

GREEN – IMMUNE SYSTEM IS FIGHTING BACK

BLACK – SERIOUS FUNGAL INFECTION

If your nose becomes irritated from too much rubbing, blowing, or picking, a small amount of blood can mix with the mucus. This can make your mucus look reddish brown.

RUNAWAY MUCUS

Not all mucus dries and clumps into boogers. Some mucus just leaks out of your nose and into your tissue. Your nose works hard to protect your body, but sometimes bacteria and **viruses** make it through. These can make you sick. When this happens, your body produces extra mucus to flush out the germs.

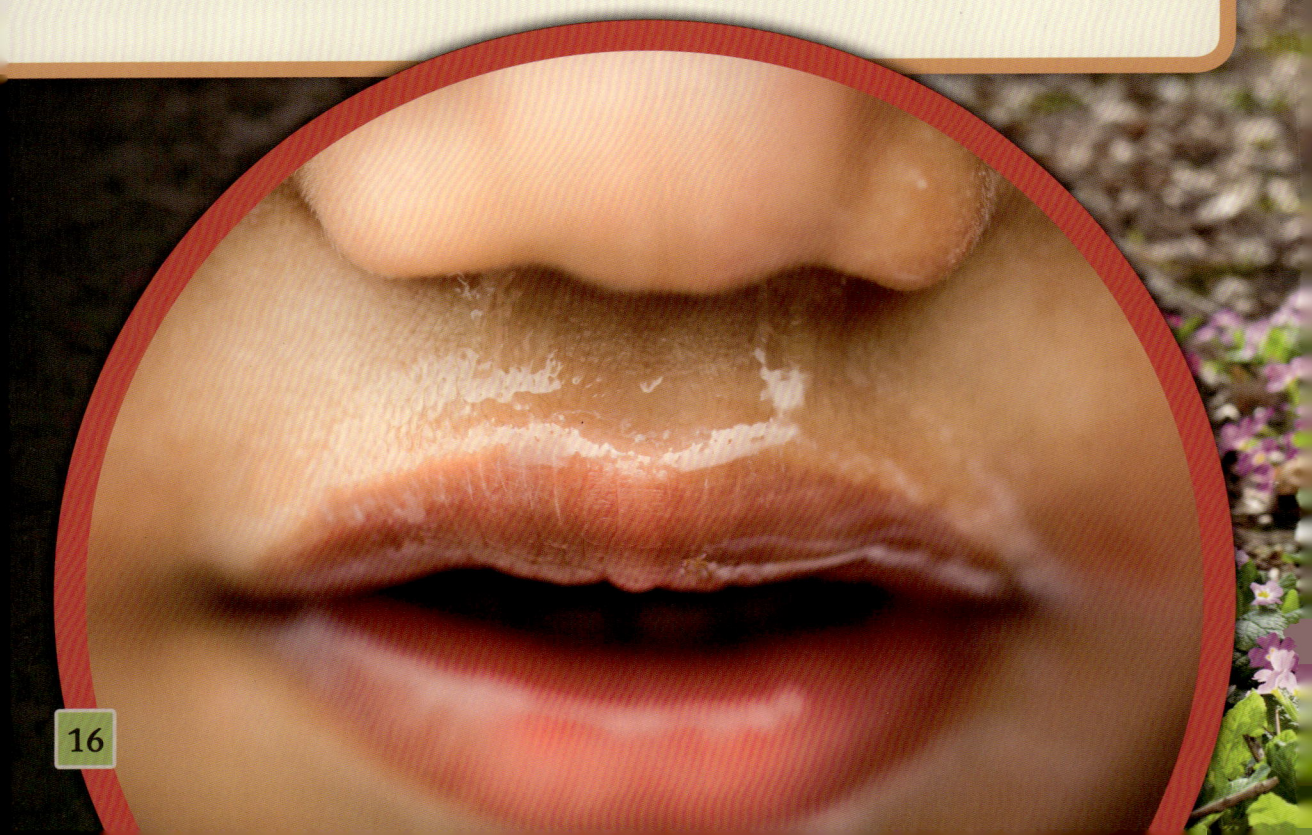

The same thing happens to people with allergies. When they breathe in cat dander or plant pollen, their noses react as if these particles were germs. Their body begins to produce more mucus. Their noses start running, and the particles get swept away in a flood of mucus.

So, the next time you sneeze or cough or sniff or blow, remember: Boogers may be gross, but we couldn't live without them.

WAYS TO PREVENT SPREADING GERMS

STAY HOME IF YOU'RE SICK

COVER YOUR COUGH & SNEEZE

WASH YOUR HANDS FREQUENTLY

19

Mucus can do a lot more than trap germs. For some animals, it can be as important to their survival as their fur or claws. Here are a few examples of what animals do with their boogers.

OPOSSUM

SLUGS

ROTFISH

If an OPOSSUM sees a predator nearby, it will roll over and play dead—and it really knows how to get in character. In addition to closing its eyes and not moving, it produces a smelly mucus that makes other animals think it's been dead for a long time.

SLUGS are some of the slimiest creatures in the world. They produce mucus to help climb steep surfaces, attract mates, and ward off predators.

y night, FISH burp ubble of t surrounds a sac. It is n why they this.

Animal slime

HAGFISH

If a HAGFISH is eaten by a predator, it will quickly cover itself in a large ball of sticky mucus. The predator chokes on the mucus and spits the hagfish back out into the water.

OYSTERS

OYSTERS eat by opening their mouths and taking in whatever particles happen to be floating through the water. They get rid of any particles that they don't want by covering them with mucus.

PARR

Ever
PARROT
out a
mucus th
them like
unknow
do

GLOSSARY

bacteria
very small living things that can cause disease

barrier
something that prevents or blocks movement from one place to another

cilia
tiny hairs inside your body

expel
to push or force something out

mucus
a thick liquid that is produced in some parts of the body, such as the nose and throat

sensation
a particular feeling that your body experiences

viruses
extremely small particles that cause a disease and can spread from one person or animal to another

INDEX

acids 8
air 6, 12
airway 13
allergies 17
bacteria 6, 16
barrier 6
blink 5
blood 14, 15
boogers 2, 4, 8–10, 13, 16, 18
cold 2, 14
chemical 14
cilia 8, 11, 13
cough 13, 18–19

dander 17
digest 4
dust 6
expel 10–11
eyes 5
germs 6–7, 11, 14, 16–17, 19
invaders 9
lungs 4, 6–7, 9, 13
mouth 4, 6, 12
mucus 2, 4–9, 13–17
nose 2, 4, 6, 8, 10–12, 14–17
nostrils 8
particles 6–8, 10–11, 13, 17

pollen 6, 11, 17
sensation 11
sneeze 12–13, 18–19
stomach 4, 8
throat 4, 6, 8, 13
tissue 14, 16
viruses 16
white blood cells 14
windpipe 7